HOW TO SAVE A ROCK

by Pigfoot Theatre / Conky Kampfner
and Alex Rugman

FOR AMATEUR PRODUCTION ENQUIRIES

UNITED KINGDOM AND WORLD
EXCLUDING NORTH AMERICA
licensing@concordtheatricals.co.uk
020-7054-7200

Each title is subject to availability from Concord Theatricals, depending upon country of performance.

MUSIC USE NOTE

Licensees are solely responsible for obtaining formal written permission from copyright owners to use copyrighted music in the performance of this play and are strongly cautioned to do so. If no such permission is obtained by the licensee, then the licensee must use only original music that the licensee owns and controls. Licensees are solely responsible and liable for all music clearances and shall indemnify the copyright owners of the play(s) and their licensing agent, Concord Theatricals, against any costs, expenses, losses and liabilities arising from the use of music by licensees. Please contact the appropriate music licensing authority in your territory for the rights to any incidental music.

IMPORTANT BILLING AND CREDIT REQUIREMENTS

If you have obtained performance rights to this title, please refer to your licensing agreement for important billing and credit requirements.

USE OF COPYRIGHT MUSIC

A licence issued by Concord Theatricals to perform this play does not include permission to use the incidental music specified in this copy. Where the place of performance is already licensed by the PERFORMING RIGHT SOCIETY (PRS) a return of the music used must be made to them. If the place of performance is not so licensed then application should be made to the PRS, 2 Pancras Square, London, N1C 4AG. A separate and additional licence from PHONOGRAPHIC PERFORMANCE LTD, 1 Upper James Street, London W1F 9DE (www.ppluk. com) is needed whenever commercial recordings are used.

FIRST PERFORMANCE

How To Save A Rock was first performed at the Pleasance, Edinburgh Fringe from the 10–23 August 2019. The cast was as follows:

ALFIE/PHIL/AIRPORT RECEPTIONIST	Lee Simmonds
JACK/TIM/CONDUCTOR	Alex Rugman
KATIE/KEITH	Bea Udale-Smith
MIKE	An audience member

CHARACTERS

The characters can be any gender.

FRANKIE - Once passionate about fighting the climate crisis, she has now lost hope in the face of change happening too-little, too-late.

JACK - Frankie's oldest friend, who loves her more than pretty much anything. He's a glass half-full type, who often puts his foot in it.

KATIE - Frankie's closest friend over the past few years. Practical, and no-nonsense.

PHIL, **TIM**, and **KEITH** are scientists whose research was hacked and maliciously spread as part of the climate denialist campaign Climate Gate, in 2009. They're intelligent, and eager to educate others.

Other characters who pop up along the way can be played by anyone.

PERFORMERS

STEPHANIE OCAMPO | KATIE

Stephanie graduated from the Urdang Academy with a First Class BA (hons) in professional Dance and Musical Theatre. Whilst in training, she appeared as the role of Barbra Castle in the musical *Made in Dagenham* (Directed by Lisa Millar), as well as playing the role of Roz Keith in *9 to 5 The Musical* (Directed by Rob Archibald). Other credits Dancer in Jack Whitehall's *Training Days* (Webseries, Working Title) and a Dancer in the Music Video for Misunderstood's Ghetto Style (Concord Management).

WILL STEVENS | JACK

Will graduated from Drama Centre in September 2019. There his training focused heavily on working from the outside-in, through movement and gesture, and included two months of training at the Boris Shukin Institute in Moscow. Before drama school, Will was a part of two successful devised shows at the Edinburgh Fringe Festival *XX* (2016) and *Kidding* (2018). In February 2020 he made his television debut in *Silent Witness* (BBC). He is represented by Troika Talent.

ANTONIA STRAFFORD-TAYLOR | FRANKIE

Antonia is an actor and improvisor from Nottingham. Prior to working with Pigfoot, she has performed in Quick Duck Theatre's *Magic Hour The Murder Mystery Disco!* (The Night Owl 2018, NSDF 2019); The Watch This Improv Troupe's *Improvabunga* (Edinburgh Fringe 2017-2019); and is an improvisor with Yes And, Minister. She previously trained at The Television Workshop, and currently attends The Actors Workshop, Nottingham.

Originally performed and devised by Anushka Chakravarti, Alex Rugman, Lara Deering, Nancy Case, Bea Udale-Smith and Lee Simmonds.

CREATIVE TEAM

BEA UDALE-SMITH | DIRECTOR

Bea is a director and theatre-maker who set up Pigfoot in 2017. She has directed shows in venues across Oxford including Pigfoot's *Travesties* at the Oxford Playhouse (2018), co-developed and produced the biannual scratch night, CAKE Night, at the North Wall Arts Centre (2019), and assistant-directed/assistant-produced Poltergeist Theatre's *Lights Over Tesco Car Park* (Edinburgh Fringe, 2018; New Diorama, 2018).

HETTY HODGSON | PRODUCER

Hetty is a producer, director and theatre-maker. She has directed and produced shows including *Yen* (Edinburgh Fringe 2018); *Boys* (UK Tour 2018) and *Beats* (NSDF 2020). She directed and developed *Yes Chef* at the Roundhouse in June 2020 and was assistant director on *Rhubarb Ghetto* at VAULT Festival 2020. She has previously run the Durham University Charity Fashion Show 2019, raising £150,000 for the Environmental Justice Foundation.

KITTY HATCHLEY | PRODUCER

Kitty is a producer in theatre, film and radio. Outside Pigfoot, she has produced Squidink Theatre's *YELLOW* (Edinburgh Fringe, 2019). She has produced several short films whilst at Oxford including *Wilting* (2019), *Various Faces* (2018) and *Bury the Hatchet* (2018), and was a production assistant for *Capricorn* (2018) and *Dorian* (2018). She has also station-managed Oxide Radio station, where she produced and hosted two shows.

CONKY KAMPFNER | WRITER

Conky is a writer and director. Her own company Squidink Theatre merges the old and new to create a unique female voice for 21st century theatre. Squidink Theatre's most recent production *YELLOW* headed to ZOO Venues for the Edinburgh Fringe 2019. Conky also does bits of journalism, where she uses her serious name, Constance.

ALEX RUGMAN | WRITER

Alex is a writer and theatre-maker. He co-runs theatre company Nitrous Cow, with whom he has directed multiple sell-out productions in Oxford. Writing projects include subject matter varying from Big Data to the US nuclear codes. His current project, *Move Fast and Break Things*, premiered in London, January 2020.

SARAH SPENCER | COMPOSER

Sarah is a composer, producer and sound designer. She writes in styles from contemporary classical to jazz and electronic, engaging with themes of politics, gender and the voice. Sarah has explored these styles further as the composer and sound designer for plays, short films, and BBC Radio Dramas. She is also a jazz harpist and music director of all-women band, *Sisters of Funk*.

ELLI KYPRIADIS | VISUAL DESIGNER

Elli is an actor and set designer. Elli trained with the Royal Exchange Theatre, performing there in *The Tempest*, *Table for 6* and *Mixtape*. In August 2018 Elli found her own theatre company, SwitchMCR. Prior to this she studied 3D design at Manchester School of Art where her passion for storytelling and creating character extended into the work she created. Having spent much of her childhood in Greece, mythology and and a love of fairytales inspires the worlds she creates on stage.

A NOTE ON THE TEXT

When we started making this show, we knew roughly this much [ ] about climate breakdown.

We've devised the show over a year. The play came from conversations we had in the rehearsal room, from research we did, from playing. Sometimes we were petrified by what we were finding, sometimes thrilled. Sometimes we just felt overwhelmed.

By now, we reckon we know about [   ] this much of what there is to know about climate change. *How To Save A Rock* is written to be entirely carbon neutral. This means a few things, if you want to perform it.

All lighting should be powered by renewable energy. We use solar-lights and a bicycle, connected to a power-generator, connected to lights. Until the train breaks down, someone (actor or audience) is always on the bike.

All sound should be created live. In our production, we use a lot of music – this is created through our voices, an accordion or piano, and objects we've found along the way.

All props should be created from repurposed materials. We use litter for just about everything.

The script itself is entirely yours to play around with. Every time we perform the show, we have to re-write it. A lot is happening very fast right now. Last year, the rise of Greta Thunberg and the explosion of protests by Extinction Rebellion meant we had to reshape the show at every turn. Since then, the fires ravaging Australia have also been on our minds. If bits of this script don't fit with what's happening around you, change them. But, no matter what's going on in the world, we think this play needs to give people hope.

We'd like to thank a few people Makespace Oxford, for letting us perform our first work-in-progress shows in their beautiful, creative building. Dynamic Earth, for providing a home for our show in Edinburgh. Junming Samuel Liu, for building our bike's first generator - and Dr Helen Eastman, for our second. Psyche

Stott, James Phillips, Chris Haydon, Grace Smart, and the many other brilliant people who make up the National Student Drama Festival team, for taking us under their wing. And we're hugely excited by the support of the Camden People's Theatre.

We're also grateful to the Concord Theatricals (Samuel French) team, who took our timid questions about eco-friendly printing and made them a reality. It means the world to us to have a carbon-neutral copy of this play.

Finally, we'd like to thank Alice Boyd and the environmental theatre initiative, Staging Change. Not only for their support, but for inspiring us everyday by their drive to make this industry a brighter, greener place.

If we've learnt a lot while doing this show, we've also been continually reminded how much more there is to learn about this strange rock that you, reading this, are probably also sitting on. Unless you've made it to space.

If you bought this book to remember seeing the show, or picked it up to see what it's about we'd also like to thank you, for coming on a part of our journey with us, and to wish you luck with the rest of yours. Together, we might just be able to save this rock.

Pigfoot, Conky Kampfner and Alex Rugman

Pigfoot Theatre

For the school strikers

East Anglia: 1

As the audience enters the space, two scientists ask them to write down one thing that they would fight to save if the world were to end tomorrow. On some environmentally friendly paper, of course. The audience should hold on to these. They will be useful later.

As the audience settle down, the two scientists excitedly draw their attention to the bike, which KEITH, *a third scientist, is cycling. Perhaps* KEITH *tries to point out that* MIKE *is missing – but no one pays him any attention. There are experiments bubbling, computers whirring, and monitors beeping, all around the stage.*

Once the audience is seated, PHIL *and* TIM *gather centre stage.* KEITH *is still frantically cycling.*

PHIL Right, shall we start? Is everyone ready?

PHIL takes a deep breath, readying himself, and then – he stops. He looks around.

He turns to the bike.

Keith, what are you doing?

KEITH *(urgent whisper)* Mike!

PHIL What?

KEITH *(slightly louder) Mike!*

PHIL What about him?

KEITH He's supposed to be doing the bike.

PHIL It doesn't matter about Mike, I need you here.

TIM But, Phil, the lights—

PHIL Who's in charge here, Tim? Keith, come here. We have to begin, these people have come all this way to hear us.

KEITH OK...

PHIL Now, is everyone ready?

> KEITH *climbs off the bike. The stage is now pitch black. A pause.*

Oh this won't do! I can't see a thing.

TIM I tried to warn you.

KEITH We need *Mike.*

PHIL Why is he always late?

TIM Hold on, I *saw* Mike here just a moment ago...

> TIM *turns to the audience, and finds "*MIKE*". The scientists get* MIKE *onto the bike. The lights come up. The scientists applaud* MIKE *for just a moment – then snap back into:*

PHIL Right. The Press have got hold of it –

> *He gestures to a Coke can on the floor.*

I reckon we've got less than five until that phone starts ringing.

KEITH/TIM Eh?

PHIL The...can. The Coke can. I'm...pretending it's a phone.

KEITH/TIM Ahhhhh.

PHIL Does that work? I mean, I know it's just a can but I thought it was sort of / magical realism.

KEITH/TIM / Magical realism.

PHIL Yeah. Should we explain?

TIM Yes, we need them to understand.

> *(now to the audience)* It's the 20th of November, 2009. We're here in the Climate Research Unit at the University of East

Anglia. This facility provides climate data which will be read all over the world—

PHIL By Prime Ministers and Presidents, by Sheikhs, by Crown Princes, by Popes—

KEITH Basically, it's a big deal.

TIM Basically, *we're* a big deal.

PHIL We are. We hold the keys to all the answers. Warming trends. Hockey stick graphs. Tree line divergence patterns.

KEITH It might not make sense to you but trust us, when it comes to climate science, we are the / bees knees—

PHIL/TIM / Bees knees—

KEITH If there were any bees left! Little extinction joke for you all there.

They do their secret handshake.

PHIL Well, here we are. I'm Phil. Phil Jones. I'm the head of the unit.

KEITH Keith. Keith Briffa. I'm a researcher, focusing on Tree-Ring analysis.

TIM Tim. Tim Osborn. I'm a climate modeller at the Unit.

PHIL Oh. And this is Mike. Mike Hulme, director of the Tyndall Research Centre for Climate.

These names could be spoken or sung.

TIM Tim.

KEITH Keith.

PHIL Phil.

They leave a space for **MIKE** *to sing/say their name.*

TIM This all really happened, by the way. We are all real people.

PHIL You can Google us.

TIM You can find me on LinkedIn—

PHIL Come on, Tim, save the self-promotion for the interval.

TIM But there isn't an interval?

KEITH Today is an important day.

PHIL Today is not a good day.

TIM Because we are under attack.

KEITH Because we have been hacked.

TIM Not hacked as in we entered our passwords on a popup that told us we'd won a free iPhone –

PHIL Because that isn't hacking, that's just you being stupid –

TIM We got hacked-hacked.

KEITH As we speak, thousands of emails, most of them sent by us four, are spreading all over the world.

PHIL They're spreading fast, invisibly, invasively. Like a gas.

TIM Like Carbon Dioxide. Or Methane.

KEITH But, in a way, they are far more damaging to our world than any greenhouse gas.

PHIL Because this hacking, this attack—

KEITH And it is an attack—

PHIL Is trying to disprove our scientific evidence that the world is heating up.

TIM To say that we're hiding the fact that the world is actually cooling down.

KEITH Remember, this is the 21st Century. We love to hate an expert.

PHIL These hackers want to deny that climate change is real—

TIM They call themselves climate sceptics.

PHIL They stole thousands of our emails and took them out of context.

KEITH They twisted them—

PHIL And then they sent them to the four corners of the earth. Now, every perniciously potty, pimple-popping sceptic with a climate denial blog has them. And is talking about them.

TIM And posting them.

KEITH They're everywhere!

PHIL It's called *(he elongates this word until it's stupid)* Climategaaate.

KEITH Climategate, yeah.

TIM This is not a good day.

PHIL But we have a plan. A plan to save us all!

The experiment begins: Now.

Prologue

JACK *is on the bike.*

JACK This is Frankie. There are a few ways to describe her.

KATIE She's twenty years old, she was born in Brighton but now lives in Bristol. She studied Biology at university, but doesn't really know why. She's funny, kind to strangers, she snores, and she has the world's worst music taste.

JACK The second way to describe Frankie is a little harder to explain. She hates looking at mushrooms, it really really freaks her out, but they're also her favourite food? She eats with her eyes closed quite a lot.

KATIE And you could also describe Frankie as the mishmash of seven billion billion billion atoms, nearly forty trillion cells and two hundred and six bones, each of which has a life of its own and yet when blended together in this particular combination forms a single being – Frankie.

JACK The chances of that happening? One in 400,000,000,000,000.

KATIE How many zeros are in that?

JACK Fourteen.

But then, the chance of any of this happening is impossibly small.

A stage, in darkness. The scene is acted out using pieces of rubbish, picked off the floor. Up until "Ignition", JACK only pedals occasionally – just enough to give flashes of light.

KATIE First of all, there was the dark.

Dust and gas spinning.

Empty space with a sprinkling of stars.

FRANKIE And then, in a chain of events that no one could have seen coming, a dying star, from a solar system that has been long forgotten, explodes.

KATIE The elements it leaves behind stumble and swirl. They form a cloud. The cloud grows strong, pulls in leftovers from the remnants of other stars.

FRANKIE The cloud is turning slowly at first, but then faster and faster, until gravity collapses in on itself. And—

KATIE Ignition.

JACK *now pedals continuously. The stage is flooded with orange light.*

The sun is born. The pace begins to quicken.

KATIE Specks of matter circle the sun, sometimes colliding with each other and forming clumps.

FRANKIE Some of these combinations fall apart straight away – others hold. These survivors grow into giant rocks, spinning through space.

JACK And one of these rocks is Earth.

KATIE Green and blue streak over the rock's surface, flooding it with colour.

And habitats.

Life grows, it is viral.

JACK Apes appear. They stumble over the rock, squinting under a glaring alien sky.

KATIE Until the rock's orbit is violently twisted by the gravity of other planets.

This shift leads to sudden, violent change.

FRANKIE Climate change.

KATIE The seas boil and the trees wither.

The sky ignites and the wet clay of the ground hardens, cracks.

JACK The planets have wrought havoc and bring to the rock catastrophic warming and freezing and violence.

For life to survive, it needs to adapt.

Against the odds, our ancestors – these apes – they manage to.

And then—

FRANKIE Hello, world!

JACK Humans arrive.

FRANKIE We are late to the party.

But we make up for it, quickly.

We teem.

We reproduce.

We emit.

We emit eight hundred and twenty Gigatons just from the Industrial Revolution until 1988.

JACK In 1988, Cliff Richard also releases *Mistletoe and Wine*.

FRANKIE Coincidentally, or maybe otherwise, this is also when things start to speed up a bit. Quite a bit.

The blanket of ozone is being torn to shreds.

KATIE People panic. Earthquakes split the ground. The rocks which once seemed so solid are rent in two.

In 2008, the banks fall.

In 2009, swine flu becomes a global pandemic.

In 2010, Toy Story Three is released.

FRANKIE I cried.

KATIE We all did.

FRANKIE And all this time, the world is getting hotter and hotter.

JACK In 2018, we're told we have until 2030 to limit warming to one point five degrees.

A few weeks later, Jair Bolsonaro is elected President of Brazil.

KATIE He calls climate change "Greenhouse Fables".

JACK In August, a Swedish girl called Greta Thunberg misses a day of school and protests outside parliament.

Children across the world start striking for the climate.

KATIE A year later, Australia burns bright with wildfire.

FRANKIE In 2022, the eight-billionth person is born.

In 2023, Space X launches the first commercial space voyage.

By 2025, two-thirds of the world no longer have access to clean water.

JACK 2026. Toy Story Seven is released.

FRANKIE It's a let down.

KATIE Wild polar bears become extinct.

FRANKIE Many other animals are vanishing into memory.

JACK This rock is still spinning through space.

It's still the same rock that burst from the dust and the dark and the light.

But life has conquered.

Life destroys.

Gases rise, and the people rise.

There is rage.

FRANKIE At themselves.

KATIE At corporations.

JACK At Pixar.

KATIE But away from the crowds and the rage and the heat – there's Frankie.

JACK She *used* to be angry.

KATIE She used to protest. Silently, and loudly. Standing up and sitting down. With clothes on, and NAKED—

JACK She protested naked in the House of Commons. And she locked herself in the London Eye when Boris opened the doors of Terminal Seven for the first time.

KATIE She went round and round for hours. Dressed as a bee.

JACK But the world kept getting hotter. Every protest, every gesture, every stand – it didn't seem to make a difference.

KATIE And so she turned away. She was sure there was nothing to be done, and her faith in her fellow humans had been reduced to little more than the two friends she kept around her.

JACK That's us by the way. But the other day, another unexpected thing happened.

KATIE Frankie's received a letter.

JACK You'll never guess who it's from...

"Dear Frankie"

The stage goes dark. Lit only by a solar light, **FRANKIE**
opens a letter, and begins to read. After a few lines, **IVAN** *–*
the polar bear – joins in, singing.

DEAR FRANKIE,
I'M SORRY TO REACH OUT TO YOU FROM OUT OF THE BLUE,
I HAD NOWHERE ELSE TO TURN, AND I DON'T KNOW WHAT TO
    DO.
I HEAR MOTHER NATURE CALLING, AND I DON'T KNOW HOW TO
    FACE HER –
I'VE BEEN HAVING SLEEPLESS ARCTIC NIGHTS ON MY TWO-
    BEDROOM GLACIER.
I KNOW ALL ABOUT THE OZONE, AND POTENTIAL SOLAR-FLARE,
BUT THERE'S NOT MUCH I CAN DO AS JUST ONE POLAR BEAR.
THIS WILL TAKE JUST ONE HOT MINUTE,
AND THEN I'LL LET YOU GO, I SWEAR.
THERE'S SOMETHING CRAZY HAPPENING – MAKES ME CRY WITH
    FEAR,
HEATING UP MY HOUSE, AND WIDER BIOSPHERE.
THE ICE AROUND ME MELTED, AND MY HOME BENEATH ME
    VANISHED.
I'VE ENDED UP IN SCOTLAND, BUT I'M HOT AND SCARED AND
    FAMISHED.
I NEED YOUR HELP TO GET HOME 'CAUSE I'M TIRED AND
    DISPOSSESSED
FIND ME AT: 58.350322 NORTH AND -3.887507 WEST.
I NEED YOU 'CAUSE MY FRONT CRAWL HAS PROVED PRETTY
    INEFFECTUAL,
BUT MY FEELINGS ARE PLATONIC, I'M NOT LOOKING FOR
    SOMETHING ... ELSE.
I'M ASKING IF YOU'LL HELP ME, I'M ONLY JUST SURVIVIN'.
WITH BEST WISHES AND REGARDS,
YOURS SINCERELY, IVAN.

Frankie's living room

FRANKIE *is packing her backpack.* KATIE *and* JACK *are watching the TV, engrossed.*

JACK You're going to Scotland? Tonight?

KATIE How long are you going for? You're still going to pay rent, right?

FRANKIE Yes, of course. I'll probably only be there for a few days – or maybe a week, or –

JACK How long does it take to rescue a polar bear?

FRANKIE I don't know, I haven't really thought that far ahead. But I'm excited, guys.

I'm really excited. For the first time in ages I feel I might be able to really help someone – or some*thing*.

KATIE Not trying to be rude, but I thought polar bears were functionally extinct?

FRANKIE That's what we thought, but Ivan says he's the last one. Which means if I don't help him, there won't be any more polar bears left! And he—

KATIE Hold on, he? You didn't say it was a HE.

FRANKIE So what?

KATIE Frankie, Boris Johnson is a man. Voldermort is man.

FRANKIE Yeah and David Attenborough is a man too, so I really don't see what gender's got to do with it. Look, the letter says to be there by seven p.m. tomorrow, so I need to leave pretty much now.

JACK *realises* FRANKIE *is actually going. He snaps his gaze away from the TV.*

JACK Wait, hold on. I don't care if we're gone a whole month, we're coming with you. Right, Katie?

KATIE What?

JACK It could be dangerous.

> **KATIE** *starts paying attention. She quickly pulls herself together—*

KATIE Jack's right. We're coming with you, you're completely unprepared. Do you even know where those coordinates lead to?

FRANKIE Well, I haven't had a chance to...

KATIE Right. Let's have a look then. *(Whips her phone out and looks them up)*

Peat bogs!

JACK Who's Pete?

KATIE Peat bogs are like these giant wetlands. This one seems huge, right near the top of Scotland. If the coordinates are right then Ivan must be bang in the middle of it somewhere...

JACK What's he doing there? He must be really soggy.

FRANKIE Guys it's really nice of you to take an interest and everything, but I don't need you coming with me. I know how busy you've been at work recently Katie, and Jack – you spent ages getting that sign ready for the protest tomorrow. You shouldn't miss it.

JACK Oh come on, it's silly.

FRANKIE It's not! You were really proud when you came up with "Clean up the planet, it's not Uranus!"

JACK Yeah, but this is more important.

KATIE I'm not missing it either. Work can wait.

FRANKIE But –

JACK/KATIE We're coming!

FRANKIE I'll pick the playlist...

JACK *(wincing)* It doesn't matter...

FRANKIE Wham! ...All the way there... For. Hours.

JACK If that's what it takes.

FRANKIE And I'll be bringing my favourites, Katie. Sour Cream and Onion Pringles. Three tubes of them.

KATIE That's fine. I'll – I'll just open the window.

FRANKIE Alright then. If you really want to, you can come.

JACK YES! Looks like we've got ourselves a road trip.

Somewhere along the M5

The friends are in **FRANKIE***'s car.* **KATIE** *is on the bike –
she's driving. Pop music has been playing, on loop, for
at least an hour.* *

FRANKIE *is singing along. Eventually,* **JACK** *and* **KATIE**
have had enough – they make eye contact, and **JACK** *dives
forward and changes to the radio. The news plays softly
in the background.*

FRANKIE I warned you.

KATIE I know and I'm sorry I thought I could do it but I just –
can't.

FRANKIE Would you prefer a different track?

JACK/KATIE NO!

JACK Oh my god, are we there yet?

FRANKIE Jack, you know we're not.

KATIE Scotland is ages away. Put those pringles AWAY, Frankie!

FRANKIE Fine.

Pause.

JACK I spy—

FRANKIE/KATIE – Noooo.

JACK Oh come on!

KATIE I need to concentrate on the road.

JACK It's that, or Wham's greatest hits for the third time.

---

* A licence to produce *HOW TO SAVE A ROCK* does not include a
performance licence for any third-party or copyrighted music. Licensees
should create an original composition or use music in the public domain.
For further information, please see Music Use Note on page iii

KATIE Good point. OK, I spy with my little eye – something beginning with "S".

FRANKIE Sky?

KATIE Yes. Can I have another go –

JACK No, my go!

I spy with my little eye... Something beginning with "R"?

FRANKIE Road.

JACK Nope.

KATIE Rear view mirror?

JACK Nu-uh.

FRANKIE River?

JACK Nooooope.

KATIE Oooh! Look! Wind turbines! Renewables?

JACK ...No!

FRANKIE We give up.

JACK I spy with my little eye, something beginning with "R" – we there yet?

KATIE That doesn't make any sense. It's a question. You can't see a question.

JACK You can if you have an inquisitive mindset, Katie.

FRANKIE My turn! I spy with my little eye – something beginning with "T"...

KATIE/JACK Trees!

FRANKIE How did you do that?

KATIE Because I'm pretty sure this stretch of the motorway was built through a forest?

FRANKIE That's not ideal.

JACK Well at least they're breathing in some of the gases from the cars. Breathing them out again as oxygen.

They look at him questioningly.

What, I'm a gardener, I know this stuff.

FRANKIE You cut your mum's lawn Jack.

JACK Same difference. That's why I'm so excited to get to the peat bogs. It's a carbon sink. It takes in loads of CO_2, like the trees. I use peat in my compost sometimes, it's awesome.

Pause.

KATIE Does anyone else feel a bit weird that we're driving?

FRANKIE What?

KATIE I just feel... I don't know. Isn't it a bit pointless to be on a rescue mission to save a polar bear...in a car?

FRANKIE Well, yeah. But... I try not to drive very often. And I wouldn't normally. But this is an emergency, Katie. A proper emergency.

JACK A climate emergency.

FRANKIE Yeah, exactly. If I'm not *at* the coordinates by seven tomorrow evening – how am I going to find him?

KATIE Still...

FRANKIE What?

KATIE Nothing.

FRANKIE Oh you are so judgemental sometimes.

JACK *(Starting to notice the audience)* Um, guys –

KATIE I didn't say anything.

Silence.

FRANKIE I use a keep cup, you know.

KATIE So do I.

FRANKIE And I never ask for plastic cutlery. Even if that means eating with my hands. Or my face like this.

JACK Er, guys –

KATIE I use a moon cup.

FRANKIE Vegan shoes.

KATIE I recycle.

FRANKIE I upcycle.

JACK Guys

KATIE Reuse.

FRANKIE Reserve.

KATIE Waterbottle!

FRANKIE Biodegradable shampoo!

KATIE A toothbrush made of bamboo!

FRANKIE I grow my own bamboo!

JACK GUYS!

FRANKIE/KATIE WHAT?

JACK UP AHEAD!

FRANKIE STOP THE CAR!

> **KATIE** *slams on the brakes. A big screech – followed by a silence. The friends are staring at the audience in confusion.*

KATIE Are those people?

FRANKIE What are they doing here?

JACK Just sitting in the road... Turn the radio up.

> **FRANKIE** *turns on the radio and the friends listen intently, occasionally glancing up at the audience.*

RADIO *(static at first, and then:)* And there's more chaos on the roads today, as members of various climate activist groups stage a shutdown of all major roads in the UK at the start of this Bank Holiday weekend.

JACK What?

KATIE Sh!

RADIO Protestors have glued themselves to roads across the country to demand that Amazon and other online retailers reduce their carbon emissions. A spokesperson said this: "The ever-increasing e-commerce market means Amazon alone are responsible for a carbon footprint bigger than Denmark!"

JACK As in, Denmark the country?

FRANKIE What else?

JACK But it's a bank holiday.

KATIE So?

JACK Well, it's a bit unfair, isn't it? People are just trying to get away for the weekend.

KATIE That's the point, Jack. They're sending a message. As I keep telling you, co-ordinated litter-picking in your local park isn't really protesting. This is.

JACK *(Eyeing the audience)* Bit rubbish for them though.

FRANKIE I don't know. The sun's shining.

KATIE How are we going to get there in time? They said it was affecting all the main roads.

FRANKIE Let's ditch the car.

JACK What?

FRANKIE Well, these people aren't going anywhere, and I don't want to miss Ivan. We can come back for it later. *(To* KATIE*)* You were right about driving. It is a bit silly.

KATIE So how are we going to get to Scotland?

FRANKIE Where's the nearest train station?

East Anglia: 2

Before the scene can start, a new **MIKE** *may need to be fetched from the audience. Or, if they're feeling bold, the scientists can try and get by with something like a wind up torch.*

KEITH It's the seventeeth of December 2009.

TIM Avatar has just been released in cinemas.

KEITH *and* **PHIL** *stare at him.*

What? It's a revolutionary film.

PHIL Well, yes. But more relevant to our story is the United Nations Climate Change Conference, which finishes tomorrow in Copenhagen.

TIM By tomorrow, all the countries present will settle on a weak and legally non-binding agreement. No landmark moment, no turning point –

PHIL It means nothing, in the grand scheme of things.

TIM And why?

PHIL Because of the hacking of our emails.

KEITH Because now every politician, every leader, every important person in that room, has a niggling doubt in the back of their mind.

PHIL If the world is actually cooling, I should have nothing to worry about.

TIM What if we're all going to be *fine*?

KEITH Spoiler alert: we are *not* going to be fine.

TIM But that doesn't matter at Copenhagen. Because the problem is, everyone *wants* to believe we're wrong.

PHIL It's the perfect distraction. Give people a truth that they want to believe.

TIM Because it's so much easier to buy into it that way.

KEITH Whoever hacked our emails—

TIM It was probably the oil compani—

PHIL Don't say it! The lawyers will be onto us.

KEITH Whoever hacked our emails has won.

A data centre, near Preston

FRANKIE, JACK and KATIE are on the train. We hear the noises of the train around them: the quiet thud of the tracks, the air con, doors opening and closing. The shadows of wind turbines appear on the stage walls.

The noises increase – and just after the train reaches Preston – they reach a crescendo. The sound of brakes. Darkness.

CONDUCTOR Good evening, ladies and gentlemen, there has been an indefinite delay placed on this service due to serious flooding ahead on the line. Would all passengers please alight here for the rail replacement bus service to Lancaster.

Confusion and the sound of heavy rain. Then it stops – the friends are indoors, in darkness.

KATIE *(whispered)* Where are we?

JACK I'm not sure, I saw a door and sort of ran for it. We needed to get inside, that was awful.

FRANKIE I've never been in rain like that. I could hardly see a thing.

KATIE I'm soaked.

They huddle closer together, gradually becoming more aware of the space around them.

I'm really not sure if we should be in here.

FRANKIE Well, we can't go outside. The rain will be up to our knees pretty soon!

KATIE What if we're in someone's house?

JACK It seemed more like a warehouse than a house-house from the outside.

FRANKIE What are all those twinkling white lights?

JACK And that noise?

FRANKIE It sounds like air con.

KATIE Why does this feel like a trap?

JACK Like Hansel and Gretel or something.

Silence. **JACK** *sneaks up behind her.*

Boo!

KATIE AH! Don't do that!

The sound of **KATIE***'s shout seems to activate the centre.*

LOUDSPEAKER *Hello, and welcome to CPP storage solutions, where we store your data away, so you can play and play and play.*

JACK What on earth...

LOUDSPEAKER *The current PUE is at one point three. No energy improvements required.*

KATIE We're in a data centre! Pretty cool.

FRANKIE A data centre?

KATIE It's the cloud! It's where everyone's data is stored. Every email you send, everything you upload onto your drive, or post on Facebook, every fake account you create –

JACK – It's all kept here?

KATIE Yeah here, or one of the other hundred centres in the country.

FRANKIE I had no idea anything like this existed.

KATIE Where did you think all your data was kept?

FRANKIE I dunno I just sort of thought it was...in the air?

KATIE Of course not! Look, these things here stacked on top of each other are processors and then come here.

They follow **KATIE***.*

Feel this side, now feel this one.

JACK One's freezing and one's really hot!

KATIE That's the air con, pushing the heat away. If the computers overheat, then the whole thing would crash.

JACK It's one big ecosystem.

KATIE Yeah, except it uses so much power to keep going. Do you remember that song from ages ago, *Despacito*?

FRANKIE What about it?

KATIE It was the first video to hit five billion views on YouTube, right? And in the process, just that one music video burned as much energy as something like forty thousand US homes in a year.

JACK You're kidding.

KATIE Nope. These are huge emitters, bigger than airplanes.

FRANKIE Why isn't anyone doing anything about it?

JACK Well, because they're necessary.

KATIE Are they? People were fine before all this. Ninety nine percent of everything we do on the internet is just stupid stuff, like sending each other memes.

JACK Oh yeah? Well what's the last thing you sent?

KATIE Hang on. *(Fishes phone out of pocket)* "I think my daemon would actually be a ferret, they're so underrated."

See! Your turn.

JACK "No mum you don't need to book me an appointment, I went to the dentist last month and also I'm twenty five now, so please stop it." Hmm ok maybe you're right but this is hardly a big sample size.

Turns to a member of the audience suddenly.

Excuse me, is your phone on?

If yes: Don't worry I always leave mine on during plays too.

If no: Who's phone is on? Don't worry I always leave mine on during plays too, let's see some hands up, rebels...

Would you mind reading us your last text? Or a text you've sent today?

They do this a few times, debating whether the messages seem important or unimportant, until **FRANKIE** *explodes.*

FRANKIE Can't you see that it doesn't matter? You were right, Katie. This is a trap. Except it's not just us that have walked into it, it's the whole world. It literally doesn't matter what you do.

We all think we're being greener right? Sending an email instead of sending a letter, skyping each other instead of travelling over for a visit, streaming a film instead of buying a hard copy, but it doesn't matter! If you print tons of paper, send it halfway across the world or just stay put and text and text and text, either way you're always emitting. We can't breathe without sending CO_2 out into the atmosphere.

And here I am trying to save the last polar bear – for what? Even if I do save him he's still alone. Meanwhile the water is licking at the concrete walls outside and we're all just *stuck*.

I feel sick.

FRANKIE *sits down.*

No one says anything. And then, as though confirming **FRANKIE***'s thought process.*

LOUDSPEAKER *Flooding outside detected, building defence systems engaged. Total lockdown being effected in ten, nine, eight...*

JACK We need to get out of here or we'll be trapped all night. Quick.

FRANKIE Katie, come on!

A scramble, for coats, bags...

LOUDSPEAKER *Three, two, one. Total lockdown.*

They've made it outside. The rain is harder than ever.

A hill, near Preston

KATIE Over there! High ground!

JACK *(to the audience)* Running through water isn't like normal running at all. Your feet drag and your knees buckle as you're thrown off balance, uprooted by the force pushing against you. It takes us ages to get to the foot of the hill; by the time we get there, rain has soaked through everything we own. My feet are frozen and Katie is covered in mud from having fallen. Frankie still hasn't said anything. We start to climb.

The landscape we've splashed our way into is dense. There are trip hazards everywhere, moss and roots and ferns, so we have to walk slowly here too. But it is drier now and the rain seems to be thinning out until we're pretty sure that the drops we're feeling are just leftovers, finding their way down from the trees to the ground beneath, occasionally missing their target and splattering us instead. We stop.

(to the others) We've reached the top.

They sit.

FRANKIE It's a shame there's so many trees, it would have been nice to have a view.

KATIE We do have a view, Frankie. Look – *(she gestures around them)*

FRANKIE It's just trees.

KATIE It's not just trees! Look, there's a whole load of mushrooms growing there, and all those yellow flowers behind us. And that big snakey vine going all the way up that oak. And –

FRANKIE I think it's a hazel actually.

KATIE Hazel then.

JACK And if you listen...

FRANKIE Yeah, there's some birds.

JACK Buzzards, and blue tits and ooh I think that might be a jay!

FRANKIE You're just making stuff up, Jack. Honestly, just leave me for a minute, OK? I don't feel like talking.

A pause.

JACK *(to* **KATIE***)* Pshhht. I think we're going to have to do...the song.

KATIE *(in an exaggerated whisper)* Oh god, I think we are...

FRANKIE Oh god, no. OK, ok! I'm happy, I promise!

Too late. The piano has already started underscoring, and they begin to sing.

"THE FRIENDS' SONG"

YOU ALWAYS ASKED IF WE'RE OK,
THOUGH YOU ALREADY KNEW IN SOME TELEPATHIC WAY.
AND YOU'RE SMART, BUT NEVER WOULD SAY
A CLOSE-READING OF VOLTAIRE IS YOUR PERFECT DAY.
BUT LATELY WE'VE NOTICED THAT YOU'VE BEEN QUITE SHY,
AND COMMUNICATE MOSTLY WITH SHRUGS AND WITH SIGHS.

WE KNOW THAT YOU'LL BE THERE,
'CAUSE YOU'VE BEEN THERE SINCE THE BEGINNING
BUT RECENTLY, WE DO BELIEVE
MAYBE THE LIGHT INSIDE YOU'S DIMMING.
AND WE KNOW IT CAN BE HARD, TO FACE THE FUTURE
 THROUGH THE DARK.
BUT WE'LL BE WAITING RIGHT HERE BY YOUR SIDE.
IF YOU DECIDE, THAT MAYBE IT'S TIME,
TIME TO COME HOME.

AND IT MIGHT LOOK LIKE THIS A TRAP,
YOUR SMILE IS UPTURNED AND YOU DON'T WANT TO CHAT.
BUT IF YOU'D ONLY OPEN YOUR EYES,
YOU'D SEE PLANTS IN THE SOIL AND BIRDS IN THE SKY.
THERE'S HOPE ALL AROUND US YOU DON'T HAVE TO FROWN,
SO JUST PICK YOURSELF UP AND THEN DUST YOURSELF DOWN

WE KNOW THAT YOU'LL BE THERE,
'CAUSE YOU'VE BEEN THERE SINCE THE BEGINNING

BUT RECENTLY, WE DO BELIEVE
MAYBE THE LIGHT INSIDE YOU'S DIMMING.
AND WE KNOW THAT YOU HAVE GROWN, TO TRY TO DO THINGS
   ON YOUR OWN.
BUT WE'LL BE WAITING RIGHT HERE BY YOUR SIDE.
IF YOU DECIDE, THAT MAYBE IT'S TIME,
TIME TO COME HOME.

By now, the song has started to have its effect on **FRANKIE**.
She joins in for the last verse:

WE DON'T KNOW WHAT'S COMING, WHAT MIGHT LIE AHEAD
BUT IT'S BETTER THAN BUMBLE, OR BREXIT - OR BED.
SO ONWARDS LET'S JOURNEY, NO LONGER IN DREAD,
STANDING RIGHT HERE SIDE BY SIDE,
TILL WE DECIDE, MAYBE IT'S TIME, TIME TO COME HOME.

JACK It's OK if you want to turn back, Frank.

FRANKIE Thanks guys, but I think I want to keep going. I've got
to find Ivan, he's only going to be more desperate in this rain.
And if I can't save him, then I'll know – it's too late, for all of
this. *(She gestures around her)*

KATIE I wish you didn't think like that.

FRANKIE I'm just being realistic.

JACK Said the girl on a journey, to save a polar bear, who'd sent
her a letter.

FRANKIE Magically realistic, then.

KATIE Alright. So. Now we just need to figure out how we're
going to get to Scotland.

FRANKIE It's fine, you can use your phone. I'm not going to get
upset!

KATIE *breathes a sigh of relief and whips out her phone.*

KATIE Well, in that case – we should be able to get a train from
Lancaster to Glasgow and then change over there to get a

train to Forsinard. It'll be a bit of a walk though to Lancaster, that OK with you?

FRANKIE Yeah, it'll be nice.

FRANKIE *picks herself up, and sets off.* JACK *shoots a glance at* KATIE.

JACK Are we going to have to do that every time she gets sad?

East Anglia: 3

A new **MIKE** *is fetched from the audience.*

TIM So Copenhagen was a disaster.

PHIL And back in East Anglia, we begin to think.

TIM It will take years to arrange another summit –

KEITH And even longer to reach any kind of meaningful agreement.

PHIL And we don't have years.

TIM We need to start now.

KEITH So what can we do? *(This is met by silence)* Er, guys. That was an actual question. What can we do?

PHIL That is the multi-million dollar question, Keith.

When you start doing your research about SOLUTIONS TO CLIMATE CHANGE *(perhaps* **PHIL** *carefully writes this onto a whiteboard, or projector)*, you'll immediately start noticing two things.

KEITH Thing One: everything you do, or don't do, matters.

Where you shop, what you eat, who you vote for, what you watch, where you go to university, whether you pay fifty pence for a coffee cup, if you go on holiday, if you make a daisy chain *(starting to get breathless)*, what you like on instagram, whether your shoes are leather, who you date, if you fart, if you run, walk, cycle, *(a breathless panic)* if you step on an ants nest, if you have kids, if you sleep too long, if—

PHIL Breathe.

TIM Right. Everything matters – everything has the potential to waste or kill or protect – and it's completely impossible to get your head around.

And even if you were to spend your whole life making a million teeny tiny calculations there's always Thing Two.

And *(writes)* Thing Two is this: nothing you do matters.

KEITH Unless you are running one of the hundred companies which emit seventy one percent of all global emissions – or if you are one of the world's top scientists *(winks at the other three)* – the impact that your actions will have is so negligible that they don't really matter.

PHIL And how can both of those things be true?

KEITH/TIM Ehhh –

A pregnant pause.

PHIL The answer, of course, is that they're both lies.

KEITH/TIM No!

PHIL Yes! They're lies! They're lies told to us by Shell, by Exxon, by Republicans, by the media, by ourselves.

KEITH/TIM Ourselves?

PHIL Yes. Ourselves. It is so much easier to believe you have no power. So much less work. Why not just believe we're helpless and can't change diddly squat. It's a perfect petri dish for inertia!

KEITH So what can we do?

TIM We need to remind people. Remind them that they are POWERFUL!

KEITH We need to undo the damage that our emails have done!

PHIL Yes. We need to bring people together.

KEITH A group of people who all care.

There is a sharp intake of breath from **PHIL.**

PHIL I think I have a plan.

KEITH What is it, Phil?

PHIL We're going to need some paper. Some pens. And a little sprinkling of our secret ingredient, boys.

KEITH Oh no, it's not.

TIM Is it?

PHIL Yep. We're gonna need some magical realism.

Glasgow

JACK *(to the audience)* The train we end up taking pulls into Glasgow in the early morning. It's raining here as well, and as we step onto the platform, I begin to wish I'd brought my hat because – it's cold.

KATIE Here.

KATIE passes JACK her beanie.

JACK Thanks.

FRANKIE Guys, what's going on over there?

KATIE Is that another protest?

JACK Oh yeah! Cool!

FRANKIE You don't even know what it's about yet.

JACK Well, it's still cool.

KATIE Right. We need to get to Glasgow Queen Street to catch the seven o'clock train up to the peat bogs. They only come twice a day – so we need to be quick. Frank?

FRANKIE I'm just going to check it out.

KATIE Didn't you just hear what I just said? We need to be quick.

FRANKIE I know, I know. But Jack's right, it does look interesting – I'm just going to have a quick look!

FRANKIE runs off.

KATIE We better follow her before she gets lost. I really don't want to be late after all this.

Pause.

What?

JACK Katie, what happens if we arrive and Ivan's not there?

KATIE What?

JACK What if he's gone, or *died*, because of the heat, or—

KATIE You're having doubts now?

JACK No! No... I'm not. I just... I don't know what I'd say to Frankie if he turned out not to be real.

KATIE We've come this far.

JACK Yeah.

KATIE We can go a little bit further.

FRANKIE *runs back.*

FRANKIE Hey!

JACK What's going on?

FRANKIE It's bad, really bad! From what I could work out, the council sold off some protected forest on these hills south of the city.

JACK Can they do that?

FRANKIE Apparently. And the company they've sold it to are planning to chop down most of the forest, to make way for a ginormous new warehouse.

KATIE I don't understand. Why do it there? There must be loads of places.

FRANKIE I know, it doesn't make any sense...

JACK Sea levels!

FRANKIE What do you mean?

JACK You said it was on a hill, right?

FRANKIE So?

JACK Well, they know the floods are coming. Maybe not now, but in ten, twenty years. Loads of the country will be at risk. And they don't want to make a bad investment.

FRANKIE So because things are bad...they're making them worse?

KATIE Look, Frankie, this is terrible, but we really need to get going.

FRANKIE Couldn't we?

JACK What?

FRANKIE Join? For a bit? The protestors are blocking the doors to the company's headquarters but people are getting tired, their numbers are wearing thin.

KATIE And if we miss the train?

FRANKIE Five minutes.

KATIE Fine. Five minutes.

They turn to the protest. Chaos as the audience become the protestors, and the actors become the business-men and women trying to push through. Phrases are heard such as:.

"Coming through, coming through, no need to pull that face at me young man!", "No no, I'll just get an uber, I'll meet you there at – oh for goodness sake, what are you all doing", "Excuse me – yes I rather think you best be getting on", and "Don't you have jobs of your own to go to?"

The friends reach the protest.

JACK There's not many people protesting...

FRANKIE Enough to stop all those people getting to work though.

JACK And getting started on the forest.

KATIE Oh god, it's starting to rain really badly.

JACK Look!

FRANKIE Who do you think's in that car?

JACK I can't see, the windows are tinted...

FRANKIE I bet that's the company director!

KATIE Why aren't they getting out?

JACK It's a standoff.

KATIE I wonder who's going to blink first.

Tension. The rain intensifies.

JACK Not now, Glasgow!

FRANKIE People are starting to leave! They're going to let them win.

JACK Wait! I've got an idea.

JACK *pulls a tarp out from his bag.*

KATIE Why do you have a tarp?

JACK In case we got stuck somewhere. Rule one of being a gardener, be prepared for all weather conditions.

KATIE And you didn't think of getting that out earlier? In the storm?

JACK Oh...yeah that would have been good.

FRANKIE Jack, this is great. We can set up camp!

Turns to an audience member.

Hi um, rubbish weather we're having. Do you want to come under this? If you just hold it here...

The friends turn to the rest of the audience – section by section, they cover the whole room under shelters of various kinds. A pause.

JACK Now what?

FRANKIE *slowly begins to sing the protest song. Nervously at first, then with more confidence. She looks to* JACK *and* KATIE *for support and after a verse they join in, hesitantly and then with gusto. Slowly they get the audience to join in until everyone is singing.*

WE STAND, STAND, STAND
STAND HERE TOGETHER

HEARTS FILLED WITH FIRE
WE'LL JOURNEY ON.

WE STAND, STAND, STAND
STAND HERE TOGETHER
HEARTS FILLED WITH FIRE
OUR VOICES STRONG.

The song reaches a crescendo. Over the top the characters narrate.

JACK As the singing starts to die down, we notice passers by have joined in from the street. Our numbers have swelled. And we're not going anywhere.

KATIE Then a miracle happens. The car with the tinted windows pulls away, and we watch it disappear around the corner. And this retreat sparks others as one by one the employees give up, and head home.

FRANKIE What's weird is no one's cheering, or celebrating. Instead, it's really quiet.

KATIE Because the people here, they know the fight isn't over. They'll go home, voices hoarse, feet sore. But they will be back tomorrow. Waiting again. Fighting again.

They break out of the narrative style. The next lines are almost overlapping with excitement:

FRANKIE THAT WAS AMAZING. I can't believe they did that!

JACK And we helped.

KATIE Guys – we need to run.

FRANKIE The train!

JACK Are we too late?

KATIE We should be OK, if we go now.

FRANKIE Alright. Let's go find Ivan.

Forsinard

We see **FRANKIE,** **KATIE** *and* **JACK** *on the train. More peaceful than before – perhaps* **FRANKIE** *nods off. Over the top:*

JACK – *(to the audience)* We catch the last train to Forsinard. It's one of those old ones that you don't really see anymore with big red cushions. I buy a sausage roll so I'm happy. Vegan, obviously.

The train arrives. The character disembark onto the tiny, empty platform, looking curiously at the landscape around them.

FRANKIE So this is Forsinard. I can't believe we're finally here.

KATIE It feels like the middle of nowhere.

JACK Should we walk?

They go to walk. They stop themselves.

FRANKIE How far are the coordinates from here, Katie?

KATIE Erm, quite a while I think.

FRANKIE It's pretty dark...

KATIE Yeah, and I reckon we don't want to be falling into that bog.

JACK Apparently people have drowned in it. *(***FRANKIE** *and* **KATIE** *stare at him)* Look, there's a path over here – what if we just stick to that?

FRANKIE Yeah ok.

They brace themselves, and begin to walk.

JACK *(narrating)* We walk down a dirt track that has guided people through this bogland for thousands of years.

Above us, the stars start to come out. If this was a proper story, this is when the Northern Lights would appear. But not tonight.

KATIE *stops.*

KATIE Guys, I think we're here. I think this is it! 58.35º North, -3.89° West.

FRANKIE Can anyone see him?

Pause.

KATIE There's nothing here.

JACK We are a bit late.

FRANKIE Maybe if we wait?

Silence.

JACK Are these definitely the coordinates on the letter?

KATIE Yep, I've checked on my phone. This is it.

JACK There's nothing here...

FRANKIE HELLO? IS ANYBODY THERE?

Hello?

JACK Maybe he wrote the coordinates down wrong?

FRANKIE He might've just popped to the shops given that we're a bit late?

JACK He's probably just having a nap –

FRANKIE Or having his tea –

JACK We could try roaring, to let him know we're here?

FRANKIE Do polar bears roar?

JACK Yep.

Rooooarr!

FRANKIE Roarr!

JACK Come on, Frankie, project. Roooaaaar!!—

FRANKIE ROOOOARRR

KATIE Shh both of you. Look here.

FRANKIE Is that a –

KATIE Paw print!

They stare, trying to make it out, becoming less and less convinced.

JACK I think it might be me.

JACK slots his foot into it.

FRANKIE Why did you take your shoes off! And why are your feet so large!

JACK *(muted)* Sorry, I just wanted to know what the peat felt like.

A pause. **FRANKIE** *bursts out laughing.*

KATIE Why are you laughing Frankie?

FRANKIE Because obviously there isn't a polar bear waiting for us at the top of Scotland. That would be absurd, this is completely absurd.

KATIE It's not absurd.

JACK Maybe we just need to wait a little longer.

FRANKIE We're already late.

I thought that maybe, between all the bad things that we have to hear about every day, there might be room for just one little good thing. But it was just a stupid hoax.

KATIE I'm so sorry Frankie. I really wanted it to be real.

FRANKIE Me too.

Quietly at first, music starts. **"FRANKIE'S SONG"** *uses the same chords as the* **"FRIENDS' SONG"** *– but it's a lot slower.*

I SHOULD HAVE KNOWN
IT WASN'T TRUE, FROM THE BEGINNING,
ALL THE SIGNS SHOWED

ALL THE WHEELS KEEP ON SPINNING.
ONE PERSON ALONE
CAN'T CHANGE THE WORLD WITH SIGNS AND SINGING,
LET'S JUST GO HOME,
AND LET THE BIG GUYS KEEP ON WINNING.

I WAS NAIVE TO THINK

ONE PERSON COULD MAKE THINGS CHANGE.
THE WORLD KEEPS ON SPINNING
AND TRADING AND BURNING THROUGH MONEY AND STOCK
    EXCHANGE.
I WAS NAIVE TO THINK
THAT THE FUTURE COULD BE REARRANGED
WE ARE WHERE WE WERE,
AND EVERYTHING HAS REMAINED THE SAME.

Underneath, **KATIE** *and* **JACK** *join in – with a mash-up of* ***"FRIENDS' SONG"*** *and* ***"DEAR FRANKIE"***. *Eventually, the friends break through to* **FRANKIE** *– and the final verse is sung altogether.*

WE DON'T KNOW WHAT'S COMING WHAT MIGHT LIE AHEAD,
BUT TOGETHER WE KNOW WE CAN FIGHT IT INSTEAD,
SO ONWARDS LET'S PUSH ON, NO LONGER MISLED,
STANDING RIGHT HERE SIDE BY SIDE,
UNTIL WE DECIDE, MAYBE IT'S TIME, TIME TO COME HOME.

I think I'm ready to go home now. If you guys are?

JACK One final look?

They all turn to face the impossibly huge landscape around them. Silence. The friends' breathing becomes slower and louder – gradually turning into long, measured breaths.

Can anyone else hear that?

KATIE It sounds like...

FRANKIE Like the peat is breathing.

KATIE Rasping breaths.

FRANKIE Geriatric.

JACK This is what I was telling you about the car! Peat bogs are like the original storage units. All through this bog, there are lost hiking boots, maps and gloves – all locked in layers of mud. Apparently there's even food preserved in the mud, hundreds of years old.

KATIE But why's it breathing?

JACK Because the main thing peat stores is carbon. 3.2 billion tonnes. It sucks it right out of the atmosphere.

KATIE Like trees?

JACK Yeah but even all the UK's woods only store about two hundred million tonnes. This is three point two *billion*! If we lost just five percent of the carbon stored in these bogs, the country's emissions would double.

And we could lose it. When we drain it, when we burn it. The balance is disturbed, it decomposes, and carbon dioxide is released.

It's like we're standing on an ancient, muddy Pandora's Box.

KATIE The Earth is alive – and she's not giving up.

FRANKIE Or he?

KATIE Or he.

A final look around.

FRANKIE OK, let's get out of here. Where did the path go?

KATIE Well, we had to stray off it a bit to get to the coordinates. But I think we came from over there?

JACK Nope, pretty sure it was that way!

FRANKIE We need a light, does anyone have any battery left on their phones?

JACK No, mine ran out back in Glasgow.

KATIE I used the last of mine finding those coordinates. Oh god, I'm getting cold!

FRANKIE We need light!

KATIE OK, OK we'll just have to make a fire.

JACK With what?

KATIE With the peat.

FRANKIE We can't burn the peat! Jack just said it's like a muddy pandora's box!

KATIE I know, but spending the night here, that could be a matter of life and death –

FRANKIE It's all a matter of life and death!

KATIE Yeah, but it's a bit different when it's *our* life or death –

JACK Helloo? Hello? Is anyone there?

FRANKIE Even if someone could hear us they won't be able to see us, Jack.

FRANKIE *sits down.*

We need light.

JACK *sits.*

JACK We need help.

Pause. Then **KATIE** *sits too.*

The friends wait and wait, until an audience member gets on the bike. As soon as they do—

FRANKIE Who is that?

JACK *spots a member of the audience, and another – and another. The next lines overlap—*

JACK Who is that? And that?

KATIE Have they been here all along?

FRANKIE What are they doing here?

JACK *notices that one of the audience members has a piece of paper on their lap, the one they wrote on when they first entered the room.*

JACK Is that...a letter?

FRANKIE Does anyone else in here have a letter – a piece of paper? Hold it up if you do!

JACK Did Ivan write to all these people?

FRANKIE They must all be trying to save him too.

KATIE See, Frankie? You're not completely mad after all!

FRANKIE Or everyone else is just a little mad too...

KATIE But where is he?

JACK *has been inspecting a piece of paper, right in the centre of the stage.*

JACK Wait, I've found something! Frankie, read it!

FRANKIE "Hi everyone,

We're sorry that this note will have to do in the place of a polar bear. We thought about stealing one from the zoo, to add dramatic effect, but they're actually quite dangerous and we didn't fancy bringing you here to become polar snacks.

You're probably wondering why we *did* bring you all here. Well, with everything going on in the world right now you might be scared – maybe you feel a bit alone. We certainly did.

We've given our whole lives to trying to save this rock, but in the end, sitting behind our desks, all it took was another person behind another desk, tapping into our emails, to nearly make it all for nothing. Climategate – you might have heard of it.

So we wanted to get you up. Away from your comforts and your desks – to show you that, although you might be scared, you're definitely not alone. And while you might not single-handedly save the whole world today, or even Ivan – maybe, just maybe, all together you can help the earth save you.

It's an impossible hope really. But science is all about those moments when the impossible happens. And after all, what were the odds that you'd travel to the top of Scotland, led by total strangers, to find the last remaining polar bear?

From Keith, Tim, Phil and Mike."

KATIE *(reading)* "P.S. We are really sorry you didn't get to save a polar bear today. But then again, that's a bit of a generic image isn't it? So now you're all here, ask each other: what would you fight to save?"

FRANKIE *has already approached an audience member in her excitement.*

FRANKIE Hi – I'm Frankie. Would you – could you tell me what it is you'd want to save?

KATIE *and* JACK *also approach the audience.*

KATIE Hi, I'm Katie and this is my friend Jack. Bit weird all this, isn't it?

JACK What have you written down? What would you save?

The room descends into conversation.

The End